PURPOSE IN THE KING'S CALL

INTERCESSORY WORSHIP
AND
THE EMERGING ECCLESIA

DOCTORS GUY & LINDY DIFFENBAUGH

Unless noted, all direct scriptural quotations are from the Modern English Version, MEV of the Bible.

Every attempt has been made by the publisher to secure the appropriate permissions for materials used in this book. If there has been any oversight, we will be happy to rectify the situation and a written request should be made to the publisher.

PURPOSE IN THE KING'S CALL - Intercessory Worship And The Emerging Ecclesia
IBSN: 978-1-948934-00-8

Published by:
Falcon Publishing House, LLC
4251 Monument Road #302
Jacksonville, FL 32225

ACKNOWLEDGEMENTS

We dedicate this work to the Kingdom of God and render to Jesus, the King of Kings, all Glory and Honor.

We acknowledge, with deepest gratitude and honor our fathering leaders, Apostles Don & Ruthanne Lynch, who were our inspiration to write this book. We honor them because they believed in us. Through their help and patience, we were able to begin to see the blueprints of our purpose and how we fit in to the larger vision. With loving discipline and a bit of pain, the blocked wells within us are beginning to flow. We can truthfully say, that we are the happiest and most fulfilled that we have ever been.

TABLE OF CONTENTS

Purpose in the King's Call

Intercessory Worship and the Emerging Ecclesia

Introduction

"Whom will you worship?" This is the most important question that you will ever ask yourself. It is also the most important decision that you will ever make in your lifetime.

You must be keenly aware that your eternal destiny rides on this decision. Though it is seemingly a simple choice, in reality it is quite complex. In Matthew 7:21-23, Jesus gets to the point when He identifies who will, and who will not, be allowed to enter the Kingdom of Heaven.

Jesus makes it clear that you do not gain entrance into Heaven just because you have called Him Lord. There is also a chance that the Gates of Heaven may not open to those who prophesy, cast out devils, and do mighty works, in His name. In fact, according to Jesus, there are those who have called Him Lord and done mighty works in His name, who will hear God say, "I never knew you. Depart from Me you workers of lawlessness."

The statement made by Jesus indicates the complexity of the decision and suggests that worship is inherently more than a simple decision to do works in His name. In fact, it is a decision that flows out of the singular desire to do the will of the Father in Heaven. It is a decision to ignore the call of every other lover and worship God and God alone. It is a decision that carries profound, eternal consequences. It is a decision that cannot be taken lightly.

"I never knew you; depart from me," is a harsh reality that many will dread to hear from the Lord on that day. We encourage you to encounter and develop a lifestyle of intercessory worship today, because your journey on earth is truly a vapor – it is here today and gone tomorrow. In love we encourage you not to roll the dice on the most critical decision that you will ever have to make.

If the concepts or terms of Kingdom Culture and Intercessory Worship are new to you, please stay with us. They will, without doubt, mesh into distinct clarity and fresh revelation.

In this writing, we discuss theology of Kingdom. We do not use the term theology, in the religious sense as many would define it. Rather we use it in the original derivation of two Greek words meaning "the study of God." More specifically, the implication of the word is Christian Theology, which is the study of God, as revealed in the Bible. Thus, the term is alive and life-giving.

Our fervent hope, in and through this book, is that you will be blessed and encouraged in your most holy faith. We pray that this book will provoke you to seek the only truth worthy of your complete and total worship.

1

Intercessory Worship

There is a remnant on the earth today that stands with resolute and unshakable integrity. The common thread that runs through the heart and soul of this mighty remnant is that the establishment of Kingdom Culture has become their focus and their priority.

Deep Cornerstone Roots in the Heart of the Remnant

Are the following cornerstone truths rooted deeply in your life and being? 1. Jesus is your "all in all." 2. You have invited Christ into your heart to be the one and only Lord of your life. 3. You are in the process of purging yourself from the world that He might consume every fiber of your being. 4. You are willing to submit to His assignment for your life.

If these four statements define the essence of your life, then you are, without doubt, part of the company of Remnant believers who serve at the pleasure of the King of Kings, Jesus Christ.

Submission to God must be an absolute in the life of a servant of King Jesus. It must also be understood that fathering leadership is critical to the successful development of your call. It is no coincidence that there is a significant resurgence of the Apostolic Order in the Body of Christ. Those who find themselves in the Office of the Apostle are not there by chance. They are there by the assignment of King Jesus. There assignment is critical to the growth and maturity of multitudes of Saints and to the emergence of the Ecclesia in this day.

Apostles are Uniquely Chosen to Position and Mature the Remnant

Apostles have been uniquely chosen by the Lord to position and mature the remnant. A succinct definition of the term "remnant" is, "the part that remains of the original." In a broader sense, the Remnant is a prophetic people who have grasped the original first century Ecclesia instituted by Jesus Christ. In fact, they intend to establish Kingdom culture on the earth.

At this point, you may be thinking "what does this have to do with intercessory worship?" Our response to that question is it has absolutely everything to do with the employment and release of intercessory worship on the earth.

It is Time for the Remnant to Arise and Function

Though it may be strange terminology to some, consider how first century Christianity "turned the world up-side-down." Regional centers of unique Kingdom Culture, the seven churches of scripture, arose and became functional entities in society. These entities understood who they were and the scope of their function. They owned their identity as the Ecclesia of God, rose up in power and functioned in their call.

There came a day in Kingdom culture when man's way became more important than God's. When the fullness of that day was established, Kingdom culture was lost as quickly as it appeared. In essence, man's spin and sin thrust Christianity into the Dark Ages. It has in fact taken hundreds of years to resurrect Christ's lifeless body out of the depths of that cold, spiritual tomb.

Through many spiritual movements, some with success and some with failure, the remnant has prevailed. They have taken us to the advent of a time of great promise for the Kingdom.

Apostolic Leaders with a Revelatory Mandate from the King

It is a significant Kairos time in Church History. It is a time that the true Body of Christ has had to make decisions for Christ and His Kingdom and act on them. Out of this time, from the remnant have emerged selfless Apostolic leaders with blueprints in hand.

This Apostolic force has in their possession a revelatory

mandate from God. The King has ordained that they reestablish the Kingdom Culture that was lost. The resurrection of Kingdom culture is imperative. Without the structure and influence of Kingdom culture behind it, the regional Ecclesia cannot function.

Simply put, Kingdom Culture is Jesus Christ involved in all the activities that operate within the culture. Ecclesia is the government established by Jesus Christ that permeates all areas of culture. The remnant is moving with resolute purpose to usher in Kingdom Culture under Apostolic order.

Christians have been constantly reinventing the Church to suit their whims. There has been little consideration of doing it Christ's way. We believe the Body of Christ needs to lay aside man's kingdom and selfish desires for fame and stand behind the demand to unify and build the Church Christ's way. Christ's way worked in the First

Century Church. Because it is His way, it will work today.

Intercessory Worship: The Foundation of Kingdom

A functioning Apostle will tell you that the foundation of Kingdom is intercessory worship. We too hold the absolute conviction that the King expects all believers to be both intercessors and worshippers. To begin we should start with an explanation of what we believe intercessory worship is. Our answer is that it is combining the two most powerful weapons the world has ever known for combating the devil and means of entering into the Presence of God. Consider the Hebrew word "tephillah' which means to intercede and to sing your prayers and intercession to God in formal worship. David made this a practice and we see that it is accomplished in Heaven (Rev 5:8-14). In Revelation 8:1-4, we also see the integration accomplishing mighty work in the Heavenlies that brings forth the purpose of God on earth. If one is seriously executing these requisite functions the integration is very natural and you may have not even thought about it. It can be song, hymns, psalms, prayer language, etc. Each of us is uniquely different, therefore our intercessory worship will vary. We believe the integration will move you into realms of the Spirit that accomplish a greater and more powerful communication with God than you would reach separately.

The integration and execution of intercession and worship represents an extremely powerful means of communication with the heavenly realm accomplishing both requisites of every Christian life. It also releases the currency of Heaven.

The powerful blending of the two move the hand of God in our lives and destiny. If Christ is interceding for us 24/7, how can we ignore our part? We are called to intercede as well as worship. Dare we ignore this call of God on our lives? We pray that this will be the generation that hears and heeds the urgency of that call. Ephesians 6:18 instructs us to engage in prayer and supplication. We are to constantly release these functions, in the Spirit and for all the saints. Intercession is not designed to be the sole work of a few select saints. And it is not to be, as many have perceived, the labor of a few devoted older church women. There is clear Biblical evidence that intercession and worship are everyone's responsibility. There are those to whom the King has issued a special call to be consumed with an intercessory prayer mission. This is a special assignment that calls His Saints to stand between two worlds on behalf of regions and nations. The bottom line, in the matter of prayer, is that intercessory worship is a remnant responsibility. It is past time that the remnant recognizes and responds to the urgency of that responsibility.

We believe, and pray that you would agree, that we are too far into time, with less success than Jesus Christ expects of us, to attempt to do it any other way.

We must align ourselves with and maintain the posture

of intercession that Christ modeled during His earthly mission. As He continues to make intercession for us, He continues to exemplify the model and the demand for continuous intercession.

Faith and Grace are Vital Components in the Walk with Christ

In Romans 11:5 Paul tells us that the remnant exists by the election of grace. Faith is requisite, and its partner grace is surely available to us on our journey. In the book of Hebrews, Christ is saying "come and enter into My rest". We are told in Hebrews 4:1 that the promise of entering His rest still stands. We interpret "rest", in this passage, to mean His peace which comes through your spirit and allows Holy Spirit to function in and through you.

The battle will surely rage harder than ever before as you take up the mantle of worship and intercession. You must be vigilant and keenly aware the battle is in the mind. Satan will wage war for your mind. With centuries of dedicated practice, he is a master of this art. Even though he has deceived multitudes, Satan's delusion has no effect on the remnant. As they begin to take seriously their priestly duties and assume their share in the Ecclesia, they will prevail against Satan's battle for their minds. With great faith and grace, their clarion call of "come Thy Kingdom – will of God happen," will shatter the gates of hell.

Are you willing to lay down your life to find it? It all starts with intercession and worship. If intercessory worship is a new term, understand it is a convergence of function. The two go together and release a sound and anointing much greater than they would as individual functions, as they ascend to the Father's throne.

Humanity is Central to God's Universal Plan

God's consuming focus has always been and always will be man. It cannot be any other way, as He created man in His very image.

We are reminded in Heb. 1:1 that God has continuously spoken "at various times and in diverse ways to our fathers through the prophets and in these last days by His Son whom He has appointed heir of all things." It is important to note that Father used fathers to implement His plan ("Fathers" in this context refers to a fathering spiritual leader of either sex.).

The first Adam was a living soul, the second Adam, Jesus, a life-giving spirit redeeming man and restoring authority and dominion on the earth. After Christ ascended into Heaven following His passion, Holy Spirit was released on the earth to lead mankind into all truth.

Redemptive Love Beckons Us into Intercessory Worship

The sound we hear, that causes us to seek Him through intercession and worship, is the sound of redemptive love. It is a call to overcoming victory which invokes worship and intercession. It is extremely important to understand that the sound comes from God and causes us to flow in His will. When intercessory worship picks up His sound and Holy Spirit works through us to return it to the Father, the dunamis power of God is released and His purpose, not ours, is established in the earth.

A Mantle of Prayer and Worship

In his powerful book, <u>The Spirit and Power of Elijah,</u> Dr. Don Lynch states, "The spirit and power of Elijah includes a mantle of prayer and worship that establishes who God is, that confronts witchcraft, idolatry, Satanism and false religion. It is praying God's will to pass and releasing a new sound. The sound created in prophetic song and insight, is a sound of passionate praise from God's anointed saints who are lost in wonder and worship in the presence and power of Holy Spirit. They are praying prayers that release God's strength to push back the claims of hell over people, homes, cities, and regions." Intercession and worship are meant to go together as an expression and declaration of God's heart from our heart. We hear the sound He sends to earth. It is a sound that creates a distinct atmosphere in which we can not only express our adoration and gratitude for who He is, but more importantly it equips us and positions us to execute His Kingdom business.

When worship and intercession are led by Holy Spirit, they cease to be an act of man. In fact, we truly stand between Heaven and Earth with a complete and holy communication between the Creator and His sons and daughters. With this posture, we accomplish His purpose in our lives and on the earth.

Prepare the Way for the Coming King

We are on earth for the purpose of preparing the way for the Kingdom over which we shall eventually rule and reign with Jesus Christ. We encourage you to grab hold of the concept of intercessory worship, and work diligently to integrate this powerful weapon in your Spiritual walk with Christ.

We will admit that these disciplines do not come easily.

Guy loves to worship, and Lindy is a dedicated intercessor. Nevertheless, we still have to discipline ourselves to engage in intercessory worship on a continual basis. We know that the radical transformation that we seek, will surely come as we dedicate ourselves to the continual process of worship and intercession.

Be Consumed with Kingdom Purpose

The newness of the joy of being consumed by God in Kingdom purpose can be ours every morning, as we daily offer the sweet incense of intercessory worship to our King. This discipline demands the crucifixion of the flesh. We are very aware that it is never easy to overpower our flesh. But know this, an abundance of grace flows from God's throne to aid us in our efforts as we persevere in the process. The joy of entering this dimension of His Glory is eternally transformational. The implementation of the disciplines of worship and intercession will begin to release seeds of revelation that will unleash exponential grace to touch the throne of God.

Authentic intercessory worship begins in eternity and prevails right through to the breadth and width, depths and height of God's Kingdom. We hear the sound that God releases in the earth and we release it back to Him. As a lovesick Bridegroom, He waits to hear the heart of His Bride resonating His sound. When the sound of our love resonates with His, before His throne, it thrills His heart.

Beyond the sounds of worship flowing back and forth from Christ and His Bride, the heart of the Bridegroom listens for the sound of intercessory prayer. Thus, in the spirit, we present the complete package given to us through the sacrifice of Jesus our intercessor.

Worship Must Be Released in Spirit and Truth

Jesus presented the way, the truth, and the life, and told us that we were to worship Father in spirit and in truth. It is too late on the prophetic clock to do it any other way. Any attempt at an alternative of Father's way, is the work of man and would produce an unacceptable sacrifice. Any attempt to release anything other than the authentic, would be likened to presenting strange fire to a Holy God. You only need to read a few accounts of Old Testament Scripture to see the disastrous consequences that such an offering leaves behind.

We are not asserting here that your worship must be intercessory worship. Any form of authentic worship or intercession that emanates from the depths of your spirit, is pleasing to the Father. We do want to emphasize that the convergence of the two produces an exponential effect that will massively impact Heaven and Earth.

Let Us Ask That Question Again

Whom will you worship? In Revelation 22:14-18, Jesus says "Blessed are those who do His commandments, that they may have the right to the tree of life, and enter through the gates into the city... I, Jesus, have sent My angel to you with this testimony for the churches. I am the Root and the Offspring of David, the Bright and

Morning Star. The Spirit and the bride say, 'Come.' Let him who hears say, 'Come,' Let him who is thirsty come. Let him who desires take the water of life freely come."

Coming Up in Chapter 2:

In the next chapter, we intend to take a deeper look at the Old Testament worshipper King David. Understanding the heart of David is imperative to anyone who desires to discern and understand the heart that worships God. Thus, we will dive into Worship through a deeper study of King David.

As we learn through the commentaries of his life in the Old Testament, David was the consummate worshiper. His contributions to the Book of Psalms are reflective of his intercessory posture.

The tabernacle of David is yet to be fulfilled in prophecy. There are indeed spiritual implications connected to David's Tabernacle that are worthy of our consideration. As we give consideration to the life of David, try to imagine and comprehend all that he accomplished without the aid of Holy Spirit. Then ask yourself, how much more should we be able accomplish with the Great Mystery within us and Holy Spirit to lead us?

2

Tabernacle of David

"On that day, I will raise up the tabernacle of David...I will raise up its ruins and rebuild it...[12] that they may possess the remnant of Edom [Islam] and all the Gentiles [harvest of the nations]... [14]I will bring back the captives of My people Israel; they shall build the waste cities... [15]I will plant them in their land, and no longer shall they be pulled up from the land..." (Amos 9:11-15)KJV.

Restoring David's Throne

The above scripture is a Second Coming, Millennial prophecy. It is already in process and moving towards fulfillment. This prophetic word is a reflection of Jesus Christ's Ecclesia on earth, flowing from a position of intercessory worship. Kingdom Culture and Ecclesia, (i.e. Jesus Christ's form of government), for the most part have been hidden since the first century. Nevertheless, their continual move toward fulfillment is evident.

In these last days, the Sound of Christ's lovesick worshipers abounds on the earth. Thus, the partial manifestation of the complete fullness of the coming Millennial Kingdom is emerging in this day. The fullness of the prophecy of the restoration of the tabernacle of David will occur when Jesus returns to rule the nations from David's throne in Jerusalem. The release of this prophetic restoration will be in the context of worship and intercession.

It is our conviction that the Tabernacle of David is critical to an understanding of worship and intercession. This concept has fascinated us for years. It is the only tabernacle that will be restored, and it is the most distinctive example of sacrifice and worship in the Old Testament. If we had David's zeal and extravagance for God, combined with the fullness of the New Covenant, we would surely realize the fullness of the Kingdom today.

David is known as the man after God's heart. Though he sinned greatly in momentary indiscretions, he always presented a deeply repentant heart, and he was always consumed with God.

In fact, the consuming fire of God that actually defined David, was his extravagant commitment to worship. In Psalm 132:1-5, David made a sacred vow. He vowed before God that it would be his highest priority to build a dwelling place for the Presence of God. David's extravagant devotion to seek God with all his strength, talent, and resources, was the foundation and dedication of his life's work.

David-A Sacrificial Offering to God

David also defined the connection between worship and giving in 2 Sam. 24:24 when he made the vow that, "I will not offer up to the Lord burnt offerings that cost me nothing". We learn from David that, if it's convenient, non-sacrificial, or doesn't put a demand on your faith, then it is not worship.

When we delve into scripture we see a recurring theme of sacrifice. Father was very specific about sacrificial offerings and the redemption that is in the blood. In David's day, the most perfect of animals were sacrificed for the remission of sin.

Christ: God's Sacrificial Offering

In the fullness of time Father provided the ultimate sacrifice as an atonement for the sins of mankind. He saw that the sacrificial offering of the blood of bulls and goats was not sufficient for the exoneration of the depth of sin on the earth. The depravity of man moved Him to offer up the perfect sacrifice, His only son, our Lord and Savior, Jesus Christ.

Christ's blood was shed once for all men. The shedding of Christ's pure and holy blood was a perfect atonement for sin. Christ's offering of His blood, allowed the restoration of His creation to be fully set into motion.

The New Covenant

With the sacrifice of Christ's blood, the requirement of blood sacrifice was finished. Sacrifice remains a requirement of Father, but now we lay our heart on the altar as the implement of our spiritual worship. The depth of our sacrifice determines the level of our knowledge and relationship with Father.

A contemporary song, The Heart of Worship, composed by Matt Redman, often refocuses us: "When the music fades, All is stripped away, And I simply come, Longing just to bring, Something that's of worth, That will bless your heart, I'll bring You more than a song, For a song in itself, Is not what You have required, You search much deeper within, Through the ways things appear, You're looking into my heart, I'm coming back to the heart of worship, And it's all about You, It's all about You, Jesus, I'm sorry Lord for the thing I've made it, When it's all about You, It's all about You, Jesus, The King of endless worth, No one could express, How much You deserve? Lord, Though I'm weak and poor, All I have is Yours, Every single breath, I'll bring You more than a song, For a song in itself Is not what You have required, You search much deeper, You search much deeper within, Through the way things appear, You're looking into my heart, I'm coming back to the heart of worship, And it's all about You, It's all about You, Jesus".

This song is about what Father wants; a repentant, sacrificial heart that renders all to Jesus. When the composer's heart heard the sound that Father released, he rendered the sacrifice and returned it as a fragrant incense.

The Extravagance of David's Offering

Consider David's extravagance and total devotion to worshipping God In monetary terms. "With great difficulty, I have to prepared for the house of the LORD one hundred thousand [100,000] talents of gold and one million (1,000,000) talents of silver... "(1 Chron. 22:14).

Consider this. One talent is 1,200 ounces. One talent of gold, which currently is around $1,300/oz. would equate to $1.56 million. Thus, 100,000 talents of gold would equal $156 billion in today's currency.

Silver is currently around $16/oz. One million talents of silver would therefore equate to $19.2 billion. So, David set aside over $175 billion ($175,000,000,000) for building the House of God. Pause for a moment and grasp the magnitude of the value that David placed on the Kingdom purposes of God!

Solomon Inherits the Blueprints

It is documented in the Book of Chronicles that [11]David gave to Solomon, his son, the building plans... "[12]all of which were given to him by the Spirit, for the courts of the house of the LORD ...[13] for the divisions of the priests and the Levites, for all the work of the service of the house of the LORD ...[19]"All this," said David, "the LORD made me understand in writing, by His hand upon me, all the works of this pattern" (1 Chron. 28:11-19). King Solomon built and operated the temple according to the plans that God had given to his father David.

David Employed Extravagant Worshippers

Meanwhile back at the tabernacle/tent, David gave full employment to 4000 musicians, 228 singers, and 4000 gatekeepers to provide 24/7 worship.

"Now these are the singers...who stayed in the temple

chambers, free from other service; because they were occupied with the work day and night" (1 Chron. 9:33). "So, the number of them, with their brothers who were trained in singing to the LORD, all of whom were skillful, was two hundred and eighty-eight" (1 Chron. 25:7), "...four thousand shall be gatekeepers, and four thousand shall offer praises to the LORD with the instruments that I have made for praise" (1 Chron. 23:5).

"[1]So they brought in the ark of God, placed it in the midst of the tent that David erected for it...[4]And he appointed Levites, singers and musicians to minister before the ark...to praise the Lord...[37]to minister before the ark regularly, as each day required..." (1 Chron. 16:1, 4, 37).

So, we see worship was released 24 hours per day, 7 days per week. Today, the average professional Musician earns $31/hour, singers more, and we have no clue about a gatekeeper (although there are currently leaders standing in the spiritual gates under the authority of an Apostle and doing so as unto the Lord as their spiritual worship). So, at say $30/hour x 8 hours x 10,000 personnel, David was giving $2,400,000 per day which is an annual amount of $860,000,000 for worship.

A Heart that God Loves

Is it any wonder that God loved David's heart? Intercessory worship is our sacrifice of thanksgiving. It demands that we overcome the flesh and allow Holy Spirit to consume us. This should be our chief passion and desire. David heard the sound without the Indwelling - how much more should we have of His Presence, considering that we have the complete package? It is time to become free of our fleshly institutions and ideas so that we can "worship Him in spirit and truth" (John 4:24) and discover His purpose for our lives.

In Rom. 12:1, Paul encourages us to present our bodies as a living sacrifice, holy and pleasing to God, which is our reasonable service. When our personal temples conform to the will of God, our corporate expression should naturally seek Kingdom Culture. The Kingdom is not meant to be just a Sunday morning worship and message in the physical structure we call church; rather it should, be an expression of Kingdom in every facet and expression of our life – market place, government, the arts, etc., as Jesus and the first century disciples modeled for us.

The Deadly Consequences of Tolerating Disobedience

"Then David called for Zadok and Abiathar the priests, and for the Levites...[12]He said to them, you are the heads of the fathers' houses of the Levites; consecrate yourselves, you and your brothers, so you may bring up the ark...to the place I have prepared for it. [13] Because on the first attempt without you the Lord struck out against us since we did not seek Him properly. [14]So the priests and the Levites consecrated themselves to bring up the ark... "(1 Chron. 15:11-15). These two priests, Zadok and Abiathar, are significant in that they represent the current issues of the Church world today. Consider 1 Sam 2:31-35, where an unnamed prophet comes to Eli the priest and prophesies: "The days are coming when I will cut off your authority, and the strength of your father's house, so there shall not be an old man in your house... And I will raise up for Myself a faithful priest; what is in My heart and in My soul, he will do it. And I will build him a sure house, and it will walk before My anointed forever."

Eli tolerated sin and his sons became an abomination. Eli saw iniquity in his sons, Hophni and Phinehas, who brought a curse on themselves, and he did not rebuke them. "Therefore, I have sworn to the house of Eli that the iniquity of Eli's house shall not be atoned for with sacrifice nor offering forever" (1 Sam. 3:13-14). In fact,

Eli's house was judged! The glory of the Lord departed from Shiloh, the ark was captured, and he and his sons died. The unnamed prophet also prophesied in 1 Sam. 2:30 that his lineage would minister before the Lord forever.

The Blessings of the Righteous

There were two priests that were faithful and stood in righteousness beside David; Zadok, meaning "one proved righteous" and Abiathar, meaning "peace with the Lord, who is God". They both appeared holy, uncompromising, and dedicated to David.

One of David's sons, Adonijah, was self-centered, full of pride and decided to set himself as king. Abiathar saw an opportunity for success in the new regime and defected. Abiathar was of Eli's house. Under Solomon, Zadok became the only high priest. In 2 Kings 15 we see that Zadok's lineage merged with that of David, via Zadok's daughter, Jerusha, impacting her husband Uzziah and son Jotham, who were Godly Kings.

Two Priesthoods Minister Side by Side

The above history was necessary to make a very important point. There are and will **remain** two very different priesthoods ministering side by side. Choose you this day which you will serve.

Are you in the remnant, a spiritual son of Zadok, determined to see Kingdom? Or, are you pacified with playing church and falling into the trap in the spirit of Abiathar?

There can be no mixture in these priesthoods. One is chasing fame and success and compromising the Gospel. These are idol-loving, indulgent sensuous Christians. The other is seeking His Kingdom in holiness and righteousness before the King, in the midst of evil and the falling away of many. The Prophet Ezekiel describes those who remain loyal to God during the end-time apostasy within God's Church as "sons of Zadok" (Ezek. 40:46; 44:15; 48:11). Discernment is critical in these last days. Choose this day who you will serve. Once you have chosen, serve with your whole heart, so that you may hear the words, well done thy good and faithful servant.

Coming Up in Chapter 3:

Identity is of absolute importance in the current epoch in which we live. Our enemy is able to deceive even the very elect and is doing so at an alarming rate. We must know who we are, if we are to be an overcoming remnant and restore Kingdom Culture in our time. We reiterate: Identity is Critical!

3

Identity

A reformation is needed in the nations, as evidenced by the loss of our spiritual identity. Various moves of God, to include the Reformation and revivals, have come and gone. But, since the loss of Kingdom Culture and Ecclesia in the first century, none of these great movements have shaken the nations enough to find and restore the model that Christ had established, i.e. that precious treasure that had been lost - the Ecclesia.

We Must Rediscover Our Identity in Christ

We were created by the Uncreated Holy One with one dedicated purpose. We were created to worship Him eternally.

To become effective in purpose and establish Kingdom

Culture, we first must realize who we really are in Christ.

What did the first century church have that we lack?

We believe they knew who they were in Christ. With the outpouring of the Holy Spirit, they had developed a strong foundation of great faith and zeal for the Kingdom. They lived the culture modeled by Christ, as opposed to man, and were thus able to turn the world upside down, in their day.

Our Identity is Deeply Rooted in God Himself

God created us in His image and He breathed the breath of life into us. When we let sin in, His eternal plan of redemption was set in motion. Initially, He allowed the atonement of our sins by offerings of the blood of animals. Ultimately His son, our Savior Jesus Christ became the offering for the atonement of our sins.

By the sacrificial offering of His own blood on the cross, a once and for all perfect propitiation for the sin of mankind had been made. From the moment of the crucifixion of our Lord, we were given access to the Father through the veil of His flesh (Heb. 10:20).

Through faith we receive the gift of eternal life and the great mystery, Christ in us (Col. 1:27), is revealed. God works in us to will and to do His good pleasure (Phi 2:13). We receive His spiritual DNA when we are born again, and we became a new creature in Christ. The Divine nature of God is injected into our being so that He can live in and through us. We become an inner sanctuary of the living God who lives in and through us (2Cor. 6:16). We are His sons and daughters and we are seated in heavenly places with Him (Eph. 2:6). This is our heavenly identity.

We live, move and have our being in Him (Acts 17:28). By faith Christ dwells in our hearts, and we are rooted and grounded in love (Eph. 3:17). We have this treasure in our earthen vessels that the excellency of His power, not our own, resides in us (2 Cor. 4:7).

The Wisdom of God in a Mystery

But we speak the hidden wisdom of God in a mystery, which God ordained for our glory, before the ages. None of the rulers of this age knew it. For had they known it, they would not have crucified the Lord of Glory (1 Cor. 2:8).

If the Spirit of Him who raised Christ from the dead lives in you, He who raised Christ from the dead will also give life to your mortal bodies. That life emanates from His Spirit, the very life of God, residing in you.

The Spirit Himself bears witness with our spirits that we are children of God (Rom. 8: 11,16). The Spirit is the efficacy of the word and the word is forever settled in Heaven. We can only change when God changes our thoughts by the word. Then we know that in Christ we can do all things (Phil. 4:13). He is the author, source, perfector, and finisher of our faith (Heb. 12:2). No weapon formed against us will prosper because our confidence is in His righteousness (Isa. 54:17) and His finished work on the cross.

His love for us is beyond human comprehension. In Isa 49:16 the Lord says: "I have inscribed you on the palms of My hands." His nature is our very inheritance and He reveals all things to us by Holy Spirit. The Spirit searches the depth of God, gives revelation, empowers and assists us to live for Him (1 Cor:2:10). Holy Spirit is also our power plug and link for intercessory worship allowing us to replicate or copy and reproduce the sound that we receive.

Our Destiny is Rooted in the Supernatural

We are destined to live in the supernatural, above the sin and destruction that is so prevalent in our temporary home, planet Earth. Our earthly mission, at least in part, is to bring souls out of destruction and into their heavenly inheritance. With the veil stripped away, when we enter the Holy of Holies by the Blood of Jesus and we behold King Jesus, we are transformed into His image with intensifying glory.

As glorified, transformed followers of Christ, we are set free from the curse of sin and death, our hearts are cleansed of evil, we live in Him and through Him, the love of God is shed abroad in our hearts, and we are changed into His image. Thus, our eternal destiny is confirmed and we obtain son-ship and will spend eternity with the Lord. This is our reward for earnestly and diligently seeking Christ, our Savior, (Heb. 11:6) – This is our Heavenly Identity.

The Indwelling of the Great Mystery

The indwelling, the great mystery which is Christ in us (Col. 1:27), should always be evident in our everyday life. God is the one who is working in us, both to will and to do His good pleasure (Phil. 2:13). This mystery, or sacred secret, allows us to lay hold of God's contract with us. The foundation of this contract is grace and faith. This allows the King of Glory to work in and through us.

Colossians 1:26 refers to the Sacred Secret as the mystery kept hidden from past ages and generations but is now revealed to His saints. Galatians 4:4-7 says that when the fullness of time came, God sent forth His Son, born from a woman, born under the law, to redeem those who were under the law, that we might receive adoption as sons ….and if a son, then an heir of God through Christ.

The sacred secret was made manifest in the Incarnation. 1Timothy 3:16 says the mystery from which Godliness springs is great. God was revealed in the flesh, justified in the Spirit, fulfilled His earthly mission, and was taken up into glory. 1 John 2:20 says we have an unction, or anointing, from the Holy One and we know all things. It is the Divine working on the inside of us that enables us to, as Phil. 4:13 says, do all things through Christ who strengthens us.

Paul said in 2 Cor. 4:7 "we have this treasure in earthen vessels, that the excellency of the power is from God, and not from ourselves." In Rom. 8:29 Paul says, "For those whom He foreknew, He predestined to be conformed to the image of His Son, so that He might be the firstborn among many brothers." We deserved destruction, but God determined to recover some by regeneration and the power of His grace. He predestined that we should be conformed to the image of His Son.

It is Critical That We Accurately Discern Who We are In Christ

The problem most Christians have in life is the failure to accurately discern their spiritual identity. We don't fully comprehend who we are and the authority that we have been given.

Matthew 28:18 says that all authority was given to Jesus, on the Earth and in Heaven. Because He indwells us, we have all authority and unlimited power. Our degree of submission in allowing God to use us, determines the effectiveness of our call.

Paul tells us in Eph. 4:22-24 "As the truth is in Jesus, you put off the former way of life, in the old nature, which is corrupt according to the deceitful lusts, and be renewed in the spirit of your mind; and that you put on the new nature, which was created according to God in righteousness and true holiness." The crowning work of redemption is conforming the believer into the image of Christ.

Paul writes in Eph. 3:17-21 "that Christ may dwell in your hearts through faith; that you, being rooted and grounded in love, may be able to comprehend with all the saints what is the breadth and length and height and depth, and to know the love of Christ which surpasses knowledge, that you may be filled with all the fullness of God. Now to Him who is able to do exceedingly abundantly beyond all that we ask or imagine, according to the power that works in us, to Him be the glory in the church and in Christ Jesus throughout all generations forever and ever. Amen."

The sacred secret is the powerful truth that when Christ lives in us we are set free, transformed, sanctified, and set apart for His glory. 1 Corinthians 4:20 tells us "the kingdom of God is not in word, but in power." The power that was in the first disciples enabled them to do the equivalent and greater works than Christ released in His earthly ministry. They were endued with this power, because He went to glory, and that same power resides in us by the Indwelling.

Colossians 3:3-4 says that our life is hidden with Christ in God and when Christ, who is our life, shall appear, then we also shall appear with Him in glory. Christ is our foundation for the blessed hope of the future eschatological glory. The sacred secret is the pledge of final glory when Christ returns, and we behold the full manifestation of God's glory in Christ. John wrote of the final glory of the sacred secret in 1 John 3:2, "Beloved, now are we children of God, and it has not yet been revealed what we shall be. But we know that when He appears, we shall be like Him, for we shall see Him as He is." The sacred secret means Christ in us in glory with Him for all eternity.

The Purpose for Our Existence is to Worship God

Our purpose and our reason for existence is to find and worship our Creator. This is true because He is the one that loves us, gave His life for us, and wants to fulfill the great commission (Mark 16:15) through us. The magnitude of such a task is massive in the world in which we currently live. But His divine power has given us **all** things that pertain to life and godliness. He has given us everything necessary to share in the divine nature and escape the corruption of this world (2Pet. 1:4). In Him we live and move and have our being (Acts 17:28).

Jesus took the keys to Hell and death from the Devil (Rev. 1:18). And with those keys, which are symbolic of authority, He utterly defeated Satan through His death on the cross.

Christ's victory over Satan, gave us delegated authority. In His name are the promises of the inerrant, living, and powerful word, which can never change or be violated. Through Christ's victory, we now possess this authority. Our jurisdiction is the earth until we rule and reign with Christ.

We Now Possess Explosive Power to Destroy Hell's Kingdom

In Christ's name we are given the power of authority/exousia, with the dunamis power of God backing our authority. When we appropriate our God given authority we cannot be stopped by any power on earth. All power in Heaven and earth is given us in His name (Matt. 28:18). We can decree all He has promised in His word. When we act in exousia, quote the word of God, and draw out the dunamis behind it, we release overcoming power to destroy the Devil and his diabolical schemes.

Through the release of our authority, the power of God is released with a powerful anointing. The anointing adds an unction of God's strength and power to our work and ministry. It is the anointing that ultimately breaks every yoke and chain that has us bound.

The anointing is the life and nature of God. When we place a demand on the anointing we should get the same results as God. With the anointing we overtake the natural and move into the supernatural. From this supernatural posture, we access the power of God and His ability to perform the miraculous.

We have all of Heaven in our arsenal and at our disposal. We have, first and foremost, the word of God and the excellency of His power, to work in and through the treasure that He deposited in us (2 Cor. 4:7). We have the name of Jesus to which every knee in Heaven and Earth must bow (Phil. 2:10). We have the promise that we will do greater things than He did (John 14:12). We have Holy Spirit and in Mark 16:17 we are assured that signs and wonders will follow us. In Matthew 28:18-19 we embrace the great commission and we find that all power is given us to go in His name.

As if that isn't enough, God also gives us angels-who are ministering spirits sent to serve us. These angelic beings harken to our every decree that aligns with the word and they work to bring them to pass. They respond to our words because they are ministers to the heirs of salvation, (Heb. 1:14).

We Inherit Our Power from Christ

We live in the power of the name of Jesus. Through Him, we reign as kings in life (Rom. 5:17). These are our God given rights. As we become intimate with the word we realize our destiny, and we move from Glory to Glory in the light and the mind of Christ.

As we mature, the word molds and shapes us. We learn to cast all our cares on Him (1Pet. 5:7) so that we may walk in the Spirit. When we pray, we connect with the dunamis power and are able to walk in rhema. We operate in the Spirit, confounding the wise and confusing the Devil. We are also always welcome to dwell in the secret place of the Most High, where we can abide under the shadow of the Almighty (Ps. 91). This is a very special place. The Greek term for the shadow of the Most High is "episkiazo".

In this secret dwelling place, we become entwined with the Glory of God. Mary, our Lord's mother, found herself in this secret place, when she was overshadowed by the Glory and impregnated with the Son of God. In this same Secret Place, we receive protection, peace, rest, and empowerment to continue in our earthly mission.

We are Called to Build His Kingdom

It is clear that we have the authority, in the name of Jesus, as well as the entire arsenal of Heaven at our disposal. Most of us, however, fail to appropriate the power that we have been given.

We are called to build Kingdom today and hasten the second coming. The Kingdom of God on Earth, as iterated throughout scripture, has the promise: "The scepter shall not depart from Judah, nor a lawgiver from between His feet, until Shiloh (Christ) comes, and to Him will be the obedience of the people" (Gen. 49:10). Our intercessory worship pleads Kingdom of God Come-Will of God be Done.

Coming Up Next in Chapter 4

Now that we have had a thorough review of the exceeding Great & Precious promises that we have been given, it is time to move on to the next chapter. In Chapter 4, we will address the call that God has put on your life. It is without doubt, vital to discern, understand, and walkout the call of God on your life. However, you must never ever forget this one thing. Whatever your primary call might be, every child of God is called to embrace and activate intercession and worship on the Earth.

4

Calling

The calling of God is very often misunderstood by Christians. In many cases, it is never fully discovered. We are all called to intercession and worship as well as carrying the Gospel to Jerusalem, Judea, and the utter most parts of the earth. Many know that they have specific callings. Some even fantasize that they will be the next great evangel or prophet. You can call yourself whatever you desire, and perhaps you're correct, but you are not a fivefold minister until you actually function in that office.

The Importance of the Apostle's Blueprints

When one comes under apostolic order, they fit

somewhere within the Apostle's blueprint that God has given him or her. If one is truly Kingdom, they will know and submit to God and that Apostle who has the vision for their region.

If it is truly Kingdom, there will be order, unity, and harmony as each shareholder contributes their gifts and calling. When the body is properly aligned and submitted, the anointing required to accomplish all that they have been called for, will be released.

Because the anointing is so absolutely critical to being all you are called to be, we find it important to write a bit about it here.

The Anointing-The Agent of God's Power

The anointing is the agent of God that enables His Dunamis power to work in and through His people, for His glory. The anointing is the supernatural presence and power of God upon us when we love Him more than life.

The anointing must be pursued daily, or it will become stale. The measure of the anointing that is received depends on the amount of revelation of God's Word within us.

The anointing must be diligently guarded because the flesh kills it. The anointing demands an intense relationship with God, through time in the Word, intercessory worship, meditation, and prayer.

The anointing is precious, and God will not allow it to be cheapened in any way. Romans 8:14 lets us know that we are on our way when we are led by the Spirit of God and realize that we are Sons of God with a predestined purpose and promise.

The anointing empowers us to do the work of the Gospel of Jesus Christ. In Acts 10:38 we find that God anointed Jesus with the Holy Spirit and power after which He went about doing good and healing all oppressed of the Devil. Romans 5:11 tells us that the same power or anointing that raised Christ from the dead resides in us, giving life to our mortal bodies.

John 14:12 says we will do greater works than Christ did. How is it possible – all things are possible to Him who believes (Matthew 19:26). Jesus reveals the secret in John 8:29, "He who sent me is with me. The Father has not left me alone, for I always do those things that please Him".

The anointing comes in two forms; the anointing within that we acquire through the indwelling Spirit, and the anointing that comes upon when we do the work of the Gospel.

In Matthew 3:16-17 we see that the anointing came upon Jesus immediately after His baptism, when the Holy Spirit came down and united with Him. Jesus proclaimed in Luke 4:18-19 "The Spirit of the Lord is on me, because he has anointed Me to preach the gospel to the poor. He has sent Me to heal the broken-hearted, to preach deliverance to the captives and recovery of sight to the blind, to set at liberty those who are oppressed, to preach the acceptable year of the Lord."

Seek the Anointing of Christ

Jesus resolutely worked in the anointing at all times and for us to do the things we are called to do, so must we ask for and receive the same anointing. We need to place great expectation on the anointing. 1 John 2:20 says we have an anointing from the Holy One and we know all things.

This is further confirmed in 1 John 2:27, "As for you, the anointing you received from Him remains in you, and you do not need anyone to teach you. For as the same anointing teaches you about all things and is truth, and is no lie, just as it has taught you, remain in Him."

Let us interject with a word concerning the necessity of considering the full context of scripture. When we consider isolated verses, we often create unintended interpretation, e.g. in Hebrews 1:1 we see that Father spoke to fathers through the prophets but now speaks to us by His Son. Some would say Jesus is all I need, but Father never intended that we be "lone rangers" for the Kingdom. If that were the case, our pride would open us wide to deception of the enemy. Fathering leadership, under apostolic alignment, is critical to spiritual health and growth. Further, it is critical for us to walk in the full counsel of God and His chosen leaders.

The Anointing Oil-A Tangible Type of the Power of God
In Old Testament times the anointing was released through oil. It was Holy and poured out upon men designated to lead. The oil was a tangible type of the power of God.

Isaiah 10:27 says in that day the burden shall be taken from off your shoulder and the yoke from off your neck and the yoke shall be destroyed because of the anointing oil.

The Holy Spirit is the oil poured out upon us that is mixed with the precious Blood of Jesus. When our faith becomes strong and we appropriate the anointing, the Blood speaks from the throne of God and our enemy is demolished along with all his plans.

We Were Made to Live in the Supernatural

Through Christ's Victory and the aid of Holy Spirit we are able to live in the supernatural just as God intended for us to do. Although some consider it no longer necessary, it is our opinion that oil should be used in ministry as a sign of holiness and a tangible point of contact. You may ask, a tangible contact with what? The oil brings contact with the priest, the Lord, and the anointing itself. These are not naturally perceived to emanate out of the oil.

It is God's design and desire that we live in the anointing. We were created in His image and we are spirit beings. Thus, we should live in that realm where we belong. Life in the supernatural realm is where we belong. When we live in the anointing everything flourishes. The anointing works 24-7 unless we step out of it.

The Anointing Demands the Heavenly Connection

When we are connected to the vine we bear the fruit of the anointing – His fruit. When the Word is at home in us we ask anything, and it is ours. The anointing is indispensable to living for God and establishing His kingdom. We must be constantly cultivating the things of God in faith and humility. Otherwise, the enemy will find a crack in us and seek to destroy us, just as he did to those who built on their gift and not the Word.

The solution is John 15:4, "Remain in me, as I also remain in you. No branch can bear fruit by itself; it must remain in the vine. Neither can you bear fruit unless you remain in me." Intercessory worship is the requisite fuel that will propel and enable one to partner with Holy Spirit and fulfill a calling with fruit that will remain.

Coming Up Next in Chapter 5

Proverbs 29:18 reminds us that where there is no vision the people perish. This tells us that the vision of a Saint of God, or of a People united to serve Him, is vital. We must be a prophetic people with a prophetic vision that has been conceived in intercessory worship. What is prophetic vision? Let's talk about it in the next chapter.

5

Prophetic Vision

We are a prophetic people who were created for vision. Vision is born in the heart of God and injected into the heart of man. God gives us a blueprint necessary to align and give destiny. Scripture says, in Proverbs 29:18, that without vision the people perish or cast-off restraint, but happy are they that keep the law, or Word. In Old Testament times the people heard God through the seer or the prophet. Today we have Christ in us the hope of glory, and by Holy Spirit we are able to hear God for ourselves.

The Power of Vision

The above information does not negate the necessity of the Prophet. In fact, God still uses that office to edify, guide, and correct. God will use whatever means necessary to provide vision to His people, be it a vision, dream, oracle, visitation, voice, prophesy, preached word, etc.

His word is a light upon our pathway, the entrance of that word, gives light (Psalm 119:130). When you love the Word and meditate therein, vision is imparted to you and keeps you from stumbling.

Vision gives you a target. Habakkuk 2:2 says the vision awaits an appointed time and it speaks. God gave Abraham a vision and as he walked it out, it was accounted for him as righteousness. When God writes on the tablet of your heart and you accept and run with the vision, there is nothing that can stop you. He will give you as much vision as your call allows.

Prophetic vision is the birthing place for all God desires to do in and through you. The vision is placed in our hearts because out of your heart comes the issues of life that we speak. As we speak into being the vision God has given us, by whatever means He used to convey it, we have a blueprint to run with.

The Relationship of Individual and Kingdom Vision

Our individual vision becomes part of the Kingdom vision He has birthed in each of us. We are a part of a larger blueprint with the purpose of establishing Kingdom culture in the Earth.

In Joshua 2 we see that Rahab the Harlot realized that she needed to link into the vision. God's purpose is for us to reach the world for Him and establish Kingdom culture so that Christ can establish Ecclesia, or His government, on Earth. Through the anointing, we have everything necessary to fulfill our individual and corporate destiny.

When we realize our call, and align with the body of Christ, under Apostolic leadership, the design of God's intended larger vision can be executed.

Vision necessitates faith and faith requires vision. We

know that without faith it is impossible to please God (Heb. 11:6) and that He is a rewarder of those that diligently seek Him. We get a clear perspective of where we are headed when we receive the assurance of faith. Vision and the Word keep us on target, as the enemy goes after our root of faith.

The epistles are letters from God to strengthen us and keep us on course. Christlikeness is the product of our life of faith and vision. God is in the business of revelation and we must remain steadfast by renewing our minds with the Word of God. The arm of the Lord, power/anointing, is delivered to those who believe His report.

Vision Leads Us to Our Destiny in Christ

The Old Testament saints received redemption from the loving Father and vision to carry them into righteousness. Jesus became the ultimate redemption. Jesus called Himself the door or gate. In reality, He is the

64

gate from the Father to us, and from us to the Father.

Kingdom is in us, we have been given the key to lock and unlock, bind and loose. The key is revelation knowledge that unlocks vision – the key is Jesus. God is a liberal giver of vision with the blueprint for your life. We are established when we believe in the Lord our God and prosper when we believe His prophet (2 Chron. 20:20). Our obedience allows His purpose.

Our victory is our faith. Without vision there is no faith. The Apostle Paul chose to rely on the Anointing and preached Christ in you the hope of glory. He was a minister of the indwelling according to the gift of grace that the manifold wisdom of God be known. That was his vision.

Jesus the Prophet

Jesus functioned in all the ministry gifts and He earned the right for us to operate in them and the grace to function therein. But the gift that was most tested by man was Jesus as the Prophet.

In Luke 4:18-19, Jesus shook the world and ensured His predestined collision course with His destiny, when He read Isaiah 61 from the Scrolls. He did not stir up controversy until He declared that the scripture was fulfilled in their hearing. With that declaration, He ushered in a new era.

Jesus came, as written in the volume of the book, to do the Fathers will. The law came by Moses, but grace and truth by Jesus Christ. Grace is the Divine ability that couldn't be given to man as a sinner. This missing piece was restored through the shed Blood of Christ, so that man could function in a divine gift.

Sitting under the prophet exposes you to the future in the now, because now is a vision of the future if you live in faith.

His Word is Written on Our Hearts

The anointing that we are involved with determines the level of our walk. Everyone God creates, He creates with purpose. We are the epistle of Christ, written by the finger of God. The epistle is written on the tablets of our heart. It commands us to run with the vision.

You can't live by faith if the Word is not written in your heart. Jesus is the author and finisher of our faith. When you see it (the vision), you can run with it. The purpose of the prophet is keep the Word alive, show the truth, encourage and correct us when we are off track. What your faith sees, your faith receives.

Our tongue is the paint brush and the spirit a canvas. What your faith sees cannot be denied. We communicate what we see and when we see it as God sees it, we can walk therein.

The strength of the Body of Christ requires all the gifts to be functional. We are all called to be what we were created to be, and He is going to keep trying to reveal what He has foreordained us to be. We are a prophetic people, designed to walk in faith and victory. To step into fellowship with God we must step into fellowship with the great mystery, Christ in us. The Prophet lives inside us – why are we not all establishing Kingdom Culture on the earth?

Coming Up Next in Chapter 6

In Chapter 6, we will be serving the meat and potatoes of Intercessory worship! Our mission is to know our God and do exploits. We know Him through His Word, by Holy Spirit, through fellowship, and through intercession and worship. The exploits are establishing Kingdom Culture, through which we overcome our enemy and prepare the way for establishment of Ecclesia by the King. Perhaps this is a new way of looking at purpose, but we encourage you to read on.

6

Birthing of Kingdom

The introduction to this book postulated that worship and intercession had everything to do with Kingdom. Worship is the consummate activity of the Kingdom. It is God's intention for the Earth to replicate Heaven.

Kingdom of God Come

When Jesus taught the disciples to pray He explicitly said to pray, "Thy Kingdom come, and Thy will be done on Earth as it is in Heaven". When the enemy comes in like a flood we must elevate the atmosphere through intercession and worship. It is our spiritual service to release the Glory of God that He has deposited within us. We must continuously refill the earth with intercessory worship that reaches Heaven and the mercy seat upon which Jesus, after His ascension, placed His Blood.

Christ Builds the Ecclesia

In Matthew 16 Jesus says: "I will build my Ecclesia (Greek word for church)". What does Ecclesia mean? Jesus chose the term Ecclesia because it was understood by everyone in that day. Specifically, Ecclesia defined how cities operated and were governed at the gate.

Christ's Ecclesia speaks to a spirit filled people that are called through the gates. Many legitimate churches exist and will thrive in this environment; many churches will be exposed and fall. Every citizen of the kingdom who is submitted to the King, will follow the blueprints and participate in the assignments of the King.

Kingdom culture has influence on the local culture. Deuteronomy says God divided the land. Each culture will have a unique expression of culture and of the Kingdom. Much depends on the place or city or nation, as all are unique.

Kingdom culture requires the establishment of protocol

for the redeemed to take their part. He intended for a regional culture to assimilate and produce Kingdom with its unique sounds, that when released with anointing, brings down the Glory of God and the emergence of Ecclesia.

Authority at the Gates

Who is Jesus? He is King of Kings and Lord of Lords. He asked His disciples, "Who do you say I am?" King Jesus said, "I will build My Kingdom and the gates of hell will not prevail". Gates represent the influence over a region. In JN 10:9 Jesus says: "I am the door (or gate)."

Jesus says He will give the keys of the kingdom to His leaders and the gates of the enemy will not prevail against them. The enemy has no keys; therefore, we should allow him no access. When we stand in the gates we must exercise our authority and our power.

We wage war from the gates. Major decisions are made at the gates. We do this through intercessory worship in the gates and the royal seed accesses Kingdom Culture through the gates. We access heaven through a gate. Psalm24:7 says "Lift up you heads O you gates! And be lifted up, you everlasting doors, that the King of Glory may enter."

We love the song "Did You Hear the Mountains Tremble" by Martin Smith. Here are some of the words, "Fling wide Your Heavenly Gates, Prepare the way of the Risen Lord …. Let the streets resound with singing."

Gates are a Crucial Aspect of Kingdom Function

Understanding Gates is crucial to fully grasp how Kingdom functions. In intercessory worship you will hear the sound and know how to not only worship in Spirit and truth, but how to execute all Kingdom functions as a King and Priest.

Father is seeking worship in spirit and truth. When we agree in the gates the atmosphere changes and we partner with God.

Intercessory worship creates and opens gates that allow

us to find and take hold of the spiritual, as well as the physical destiny for our cities. Carrying the Glory, which is refueled and maintained through intercessory worship, is prerequisite to standing in the gates. Glory brings life and joy, whereas the lack of glory produces death.

When the Christian hears the sound and presses in with intercessory worship, a new atmosphere and realm of Glory opens. When that happens, His Kingdom can be carried through the gates and effect change in the cities.

The Perils of Church-anity

Ecclesia is regional because natural culture is regional and unique to the region. It will remain unique to the region when the aspects of Kingdom are assimilated. Most churches today completely ignore Kingdom. We are of the opinion that the devil is rather happy with Church-anity because in such a scenario, the Church is weak, untrained, and living far below purpose and victory.

Jesus is the King and He is waiting for us to hear the sound and establish Kingdom culture after His pattern. His Kingdom is first and foremost spiritual, so it is required that one be born again of the Spirit, in order to see or experience Kingdom.

We are a body, the Body of Christ, each unique with a defined purpose and an assignment. Some are called to be a gift to the body, they are 5-fold leaders that prepare the Body to function in Ecclesia. Church-anity has significantly bastardized the concept. Mistakes have been made by the church, that have repeated themselves throughout history. They have impeded and precluded the establishment of Kingdom Culture.

Church-anity has chosen its own heroes and perpetuated a false belief among Christians. They have created a culture that has seduced Christians to believe that they must chase conferences and superstar preachers and teachers. While this has had its merits, it has also created significant division and damage to the Body.

There is only one Ultimate, one Superstar, in the Kingdom. He is the King, Jesus Christ.

There is a Demand for Kingdom Leaders

The establishment of the Kingdom demands Kingdom leaders. Kingdom leaders are chosen, anointed, and appointed by the King.

This orderly process is known as Apostolic Order. It was obtained from The King by the Apostles. These apostles were given blueprints and they functioned very well in getting the Gospel to the known world of that time.

Can we create Apostolic Order in this day? Can We, the People of God, get out of the way and allow Christ to Build His Ecclesia?

Will it happen? We say that it will because it is the purpose and will of God. The blueprint is clearly defined and patterned by Jesus in New Testament Scripture.

Will it happen on our watch? We believe that it will. Our faith and intercession are purposed for a powerful reset that will usher in Kingdom Culture.

The timing and circumstances are ripe with the best posture available since the first century. The remnant is attentive. They are hearing the sound.

We were Listening for a Different Sound.

Not too long ago, we heard the sound and Holy Spirit calling us to something different. We did not know what it was, but we did know that something deep inside our spirit did not resonate with churches where we had worshiped. Though these were led by anointed and sincere leaders to whom we were submitted, we just did not fit and therefore, were not producing fruit.

Our exits were properly executed on good terms, in love and blessing. Our exit was for one reason and one reason only. We moved because our spirits were not resonating with the "sound" that the church was producing. We have no judgement or condemnation in our hearts. We finally heard Father's sound and had to replicate. The sound resonated in us and was drawing us to a Kingdom center to be trained and released in our destined purpose.

We can report that we heard correctly and have become shareholders of what some may call Church. More specifically, the founders call our Body a Freedom Center for an emerging Ecclesia. We have become a part of this emerging regional Ecclesia known as Freedom House. Our submission to Apostolic Order and the Kingdom Culture of the House has begun to identify our purpose and bring growth with fellow leaders in the House.

Submission to the Order of the House is Key

Submission is a very significant key to kingdom. It is the King who chooses true Apostles, gives them the ability to provide fathering leadership, and place the believer in their call.

If you are thinking that there are those in the Body of Christ that claim to be Apostles and are not, you are correct. But if you are submitted to Holy Spirit, you will know it when you see Apostolic fruit. The true Apostle is submitted to the King and marked by humility.

Though submission to the Apostle's fathering leadership may be painful, stripping away the flesh is always painful. Submission to the fathering leader and following his defined pathway for you, results in immense personal and spiritual growth. It also equips you to step into the call of God for your life. It is our experience that this process is closest thing to truly experiencing the love of Christ.

Another key outcome of submitting to and growing in the Ecclesia is that an abundance of spiritual fruit is produced. Every shareholder knows their function. They are taught, counseled, encouraged and nurtured in their function in the Body.

Although there may be many shareholders in the Ecclesia, each with a different, well-defined function, they are diligent in their work and harmonious in relationship with all. They do the work of the ministry together. They labor in consonance and unity honoring all members of the regional body. The result is Apostolic Order and emergence of Kingdom Culture.

The Heartbeat of Kingdom Culture

Worship and intercession are the heartbeat and basis of Kingdom Culture. We are positioned for a great awakening. It will be vital in that time, that we have solid kingdom leaders in place. They must be leaders who know their call, their function, and are willingly submitted to apostolic order.

Kingdom leaders do not become Kingdom leaders by reading a book, getting a degree, or networking with a "good ole boy" order within the body. There is only one pathway for the birth of a Kingdom Leader.

Kingdom leaders become leaders through their willing immersion into intercessory worship. It is their life source, their power plug. Without it, they would be like the man without the wedding garment in Matthew 22:11-12. There would be clear evidence they were "imposters." They would surely not prevail in the culture of the Kingdom.

In Acts 2 we see that Holy Spirit's indwelling manifested in power. It was the Spirit that empowered the first century Apostles to establish Kingdom Culture and Ecclesia throughout their known world.

The Apostolic Order is a Living Institution,

Yes, there are those today who would say, "But, Doctors the Apostles died and all these crazy things that you espouse died with them."

And we would say to them, "No, Apostolic Order is a living institution of our Lord, that man has attempted to kill so that he could receive the glory instead of the One to whom all Glory and Honor is due." Christians have been given the fullness of Holy Spirit power. The great men and women of faith in Hebrews 12 longed from afar to see our day. As we stand on the edge of it, we are in awe of the moving of the Sovereign Hand of our God as He births His Ecclesia.

The Fullness of Ecclesia comes in the Fullness of Time. Father desires fullness and increase in everything. The accumulation of restoration is at its fullest point in time. We have so much available today as the restoration of all things comes together. Of course we speak of the growth of the 5-fold ministry, prayer and evangelistic movements, etc. Failures do not limit full restoration. Proper functioning is maturity, and time brings maturity. We have an opportunity to make a powerful impact on Ecclesia.

There is a Need for True Leaders in the Emerging Ecclesia

What has always been missing are leaders. This day, as the Church transitions towards the Ecclesia model, there is more opportunity, equipping, leaders, exercising of gifts, etc. than ever before. If we can prepare kingdom statesmen, we will pave the way for purpose of Ecclesia. Fullness of Ecclesia exists, in the maturation of power and function, in the hands of functional leadership.

Maturity will bring effectiveness and influence and, according to Apostle Don Lynch, this is what kingdom people worldwide are starving to see.

It is important to know that nothing has been lost that can't be restored by the increase of maturing intercession. Revivals that touch culture impact nations. Apostolic/Prophetic Kingdom seeking leadership tells us that 2018 and 2019 are years of open doors/gates for the remnant to become established and viable. They believe that in the 2020's the USA and Nations are going to get it right in establishing Kingdom Culture.

We Must Build Ecclesia According to Christ's Blueprints
When Jesus ascended, He left us with all that is necessary to build Ecclesia, as well as a mandate to do all that He had commanded us to do. Jesus is as involved as ever but we have, in many places, shut Him out and redefined how He should operate. Church-anity is clearly operating outside of the parameters that Christ has established.

Earth's culture should be a copy of Heaven's culture. The Father's heart is Nations. The blueprints exist for a Regional Ecclesia that fits together to form the Kingdom fabric of the Nation.

Jesus is the inheritor of the nations which He secured through His cross and resurrection. Without secured personal property rights kingdom culture is impossible.

Righteousness always follows kingdom culture. The wicked lose their grip in kingdom culture. All land belongs to God. Spiritual dominion and principles of kingdom culture prosper and increase toward fullness. As remnant people, we need to take our inheritance and bring kingdom culture to cities such as ours.

We Must Grab Hold of Our Generational Inheritance

Each generation receives an inheritance of purpose. We have an opportunity to separate royal seed and tares and see a harvest of purpose. The Seven Mountain understanding of culture, as well as other revelatory concepts, are moving toward and allowing understanding of Apostolic Order and kingdom culture. We are moving to an effectiveness that will remind of us of the Book of Acts. We need to look at the hope we've been given in this great darkness that we now find ourselves in. As God is moving us forward, Church-anity is moving in the opposite direction. It remains in denial of God's miraculous and sovereign works today. We are positioned for a great spiritual awakening. It is critical that we have kingdom leaders in place to lead the way to the establishment of Christ's Ecclesia on Earth, as it is in Heaven.

We Must Flood the Earth with Kingdom Culture and Purpose

Jesus redeemed the Earth. It is His planet and we **must** take it and occupy it, for this is our purpose. In the near future, we will see amazing battles in the spirit. The years of 2018-20 will see radical shifts that, if we are prepared, will position to establish Kingdom. Prophetic people will discern a sound that develops an affinity with the land. When we are in our place with the affinity of the sound and the land, the ensuing function will be Kingdom.

As the tares are removed from the Royal Seed, the people are beginning to be drawn to the sound that will resonate in tune with the land. It will become a powerful and unique expression of Kingdom Culture that will usher in Ecclesia.

Ecclesia Makes No Place for, "What's in It for Me?"

A grave concern in the face of the advancement of the Ecclesia, is that Christians are looking for "what's in it for me". This is not how Jesus defined or intended Ecclesia. Ecclesia is about the unity of God's people, properly aligned regionally, nationally, and globally. When we get dialed in we will see God's favor, and with correct order and positioning of the Body, it will begin to function for The King. Scripture speaks of regional ecclesia with leaders positioned in the gates. The regions are all unique, therefore it will sound different in the various regions. The first impact is cultural clash.

A Time of Mega Grace and Air Superiority

Apostle Dutch Sheets says we are coming into a season of Mega Grace, with air superiority. This will facilitate the Ecclesia's ability to overcome many obstacles to growth. As a former military leaders, we can tell you this is big and critical to the acquisition of the land and defeat of the enemy, both in the physical and the spiritual world. The spiritual world is more real than the physical.

Christ: Our Only Source for Personal and Cultural Identity

Jesus is the only source for authentic identity in the process. With purpose moving toward fulfillment, the spiritual influence will increase to a point where the culture of the Kingdom will begin to impact the existing culture and cause a cultural shift or reset.

Sincere Christians will hear the sound as it begins to mature and increase. They will be drawn to their unique position and find it easy to submit to Apostolic Order. They will possess a willingness to be fathered, and they will faithfully accept their share in executing Kingdom Culture.

We are thrilled to be a part of this movement of Kingdom Culture. Over the past year, we have received frequent comments and questions such as "wow you guys have grown" or "what has happened to you?". Worship/intercession, in copious amounts has allowed God to place us on course for the destiny that He purposed for our lives. After years of searching, faithfulness in intercessory worship birthed purpose and blocked wells began to open up and flow out of us.

Though there was an initial shock, we found it to be as natural as ducks to water because it is the intent and will of God that is finally being restored. We have set our face as a flint to fulfill our destiny in the Kingdom of God and the Nations.

Our hearts desire for you is that you mature in intercessory worship or if you are mature in this key area, that you reach new levels. Are you hearing the sound? Holy Spirit will reveal Kingdom, and the fire will begin to consume you and propel you to all that God designed for your life. Come Thy Kingdom – Be Done Thy Will on earth as it is in Heaven.

Coming Up in the Chapter Seven

Intercessory worship seeks fullness. Creation groans for fullness. As we approach the fullness of time, already knowing the outcome, intercessory worship is the most effective means for being and remaining strong in the victory that we are already assured.

7

Fullness of Time

Fullness is the design and desire of God. We were created for fullness. We were created in His image and are co-heirs, with Jesus Christ, of the Kingdom. We create with our words, just as our Creator created with His words. The Great Mystery, Christ in us, alone should awaken our identity. Additionally, Jesus gave us His Glory.

You may ask, "Doctors, do you really believe all this stuff?" Yes, we do – it is written in the Bible, the Word of God.

Becoming an Effective Kingdom Leader

To position yourself to be an effective Kingdom leader it is necessary to seamlessly integrate the complete canon of scripture in such a way that you solidify unshakable faith.

Jesus answered Satan's taunts and temptations with Scripture. We should be prepared to do the same. The great heroes of the faith in Hebrews 11, without the massive revelatory knowledge and power available to us, believed by faith for the promises of God. We remind of all that is available to the body to encourage Christians to set aside differences and begin living for Kingdom.

Man's way has failed, and it is time to do it God's way. The starting point and endpoint is intercessory worship. Christ, after all, ever lives to intercede for us. His is a 24/7 effort. This is the model that will birth Ecclesia.

With all of our understanding, why are we so far off course? It is time to press in and pray through as we accelerate into the most exciting Day that History has ever known. Because we are so close to the end, the enemy is raging, spewing hatred, and deceiving many. The remnant must boldly thrust into the darkness with the glorious light of the Gospel.

Darkness & Light Will Engage in a Great Battle

In the near future, as we approach the end of the age, we are going to see a great battle waged between the Kingdom of Light and the kingdom of darkness. Light always prevails against darkness, but the enemy will deceive many, even the very elect.

Our first line of defense, as we engage in battle, is intercessory worship. The kingdom of darkness will replicate light and deceive many into false worship. The remnant overcomes and is victorious by the Blood of the Lamb and the word of their testimony. Satan will use "false prophetic" preaching, that will be confirmed with false signs and wonders. He will even work to raise up his "prophetic" worship and prayer movement. The coming of the lawless one (Antichrist) is according to the working of Satan, with all power, signs, and lying wonders, and with all unrighteous deception (2 Thes. 2:9-10).

The False Image and The Mark of the Beast

The False Prophet's commitment is to raise up a global worship and prayer movement. This False Prophet is granted power to give breath to the image of the beast...to cause as many as would not worship the image...to be killed. He causes all...rich and poor, free and slave, to receive a mark on their right hand or on their forehead, so that no one may buy or sell except he has the mark... (Rev. 13:15-17).

The image and mark of the Beast will be two components that will mobilize and finance the Antichrist's global worship movement. The image of the Beast will mobilize Antichrist's worshippers and penalize resistors. The mark of the Beast will provide economic support for the Antichrist's worship movement and will penalize resistors. Satan will masterfully utilize worship to achieve his deception, for he, as Lucifer, was once the Father's chief musician in Heaven, before he rebelled and fell from Heaven.

The False Prophet Will Perform Signs and Wonders

The False Prophet will perform great signs that are great in power. These works will also be great in significance and deception (Rev. 16:14; 19:20; 13:14; Matt. 24:11, 24; Mark. 13:22; 2 Thess. 2:9). We speculate that the miracles are likely to occur in large Antichrist worship events.

The False Prophet's primary goal is to raise up a

worldwide worship movement in which Satan and the Antichrist are worshipped (Rev. 13:4, 8, 12, 15). " And he, the False Prophet, will exercise all of the authority of the first beast (Antichrist) in his presence and cause the Earth to worship the first beast (Antichrist)...He performs great signs, making fire come down from heaven on the earth in the sight of men" (Rev. 13:12-13).

God's Covenant with His People Will Be Their Safety in That Day

Have no fear for God has established Covenant with those that accept life in Christ. He said, "I will not," and He absolutely cannot and will not violate His Word. His Covenant with us is absolute. He brings our fullness out of His fullness. As on the day of Pentecost, all that is required of us is to believe, obey, and receive. The Old Testament Patriarchs longed to see the day in which we

96

live. As we write we are mere days away from 2018 and have entered into the year 5778 in the Hebrew calendar. It has been proclaimed by the prophets as the year of the open door. Apostle Dutch Sheets has prophesied that we are entering a period of "Mega Grace" and a huge reset as we approach the 2020's.

The Lord showed us that there is significance to the number "8" and reminded us of the one-sided covenant He made with Abraham (Genesis 15). The covenant was actually made with and for Abraham. God had to put Abraham asleep so that he could survive His Presence. Abraham prepared the blood sacrifice prescribed by God and laid it out in the manner of the time so that cutting of covenant could be accomplished.

In those days, the participants of a covenant would walk a figure eight amongst the sacrifice, while reciting the covenant they were entering into.

The Almighty walked it alone as Abraham slept. "When God made a promise to Abraham, because He could vow by no one greater, He vowed by Himself" (Heb. 6:13-18). This was the yes and amen of God where the immutable promise was made that Abraham would see from afar, and the road to redemption from Adam's failure.

This and other Old Testament Blood Covenants were types and shadows. These became reality in the final and perfect sacrifice of Jesus Christ, establishing in His Blood the new and unending covenant. We are coming into a time of inheritance of the fullness of the immutable promises of God.

The Door is Open & Mega Grace is Available

We believe the "8" is a reminder of covenant signifying that the door is open with "Mega Grace" available to establish the Kingdom Culture that will be necessary for an end time push of the Gospel to the Nations.

The body of Christ is awakening and receiving God's favor. The wealth of the wicked is transferring to the righteous. We see the beginnings of the coming of the Millennial prophesy of Haggai concerning the latter house: "For thus says the LORD of Hosts: Once more, in a little while, and I will shake the heavens and earth, the sea and dry *land*; And I will shake all the nations, and they will come with the wealth of all nations shall come: and I will fill this house with glory, says the LORD of Hosts. The silver is Mine, and the gold is Mine, says the LORD of Hosts. The glory of this latter house will be greater than of the former, says the LORD of Hosts. And in this place, I will give peace, says the LORD of Hosts" (Hag. 2:6-9). There is a good portion of important meat in this prophesy that we need to understand and appropriate in this hour.

Financing the End Time Harvest

The silver and the gold belong to the Kingdom and will be needed to finance the end time harvest of souls. Our good friend, Prophet Joshua Todd, received revelation on this area and has published a book entitled "Inheritance Invasion." This is a book that we believe should be required reading for all Kingdom leaders.

In the book, Prophet Todd explains how the enemy has stolen our inheritance and how we can get it back with cascading interest. God has shown Prophet Todd that "Glory is one of the greatest vehicles for expediting the inheritance invasion. The Glory of God is a revelation of His character manifested. Glory is the atmosphere in which God's manifested character invades His church". We are beginning to see, on the global scene, massive amounts of wealth beginning to transfer from the wealth stolen from the righteous, that has been hoarded by Satan and his minions.

Prophet Todd brings clarity to the fact that we all have an inheritance that we need to take from the enemy with interest, for everything that it did for him and for what it could have produced in the hand of the righteous.

God Is in Control

Father is in control. Father has said yes and amen. When we see with spiritual eyes, a glimpse of the day in which we are privileged to live, we will see revelation of the Kingdom unfolding before us. The importance of our part is the work of intercessory worship that moves the hand of God.

Romans 8 tells us that creation awaits anxiously, or groans for the release of bondage that will come with the manifestation of the sons of God.

Intercessory worship is the key to unlocking life for the remnant. While fear grips the hearts of many, the remnant will gain strength and finish victorious. Those who know their God will be strong and do exploits (Dan 11:32). Whatever is born of God overcomes the world: and this is the victory that overcomes the world, even our faith (1 John 5:4).

The question of the ages will always remain - whom will you worship? We will echo what Joshua said: "...choose today whom you will serve...Yet as for me and my house, we will serve the Lord" (Josh. 24:15). We bless you in the name of the King of Kings, Jesus Christ, and it is our fervent prayer that we have encouraged in you a hunger for intercessory worship and a desire to embrace Kingdom Culture.

EPILOGUE

God doesn't change – He is the same yesterday, today and forever. Man changes constantly in response to the influences that surround him. The Body of Christ is intended to move from Glory to Glory as we allow Holy Spirit to lead us in conformation to the image of God.

We are living in the most amazing epoch of time ever in God. This period of acceleration brings new change daily. We would be remiss if we went to print with this book without acknowledging the initiation of a turnaround in America that we have just spiritually and prophetically witnessed. In the period of a week God has orchestrated a series of events making the most profound statement since His Son and Holy Spirit came on the scene. Our Apostolic leaders, led by Apostle Dutch Sheets, have just completed a significant event in Washington, DC, termed "Turnaround", February 22-24, 2018, to declare the turnaround of the United States of America to her roots and to usher in a new era in the Kingdom of God. Prophet Chuck Pierce stated that unless you are 105+ years old, the Turnaround Conference in February of 2018 would mark the first new era of time in your lifetime on this earth. That is a very significant statement.

It is very significant that Father issued so many signs in this powerful moment of time. Billy Graham ended his earthly mission passing his mantle to the next men of God to carry. Artifacts proving the existence of Old Testament prophets were uncovered by archeologists, etc. God is speaking to us all very clearly in these last hours. Awaken remnant – this is the hour we were destined to and made for.

Let intercessory worship guide you into this hour of fulfillment of the Kingdom of God. He will lead you into all truth.

Make Kingdom a priority! If we remain washed with the pure water of the Word, align in apostolic order and stay in communication with the King, we are convinced the remnant will achieve our purpose. Kingdom of God come! Will of God be done on earth as it is in Heaven.

www.ingramcontent.com/pod-product-compliance
Lightning Source LLC
Chambersburg PA
CBHW061750020426
42331CB00006B/1412